A tattered coat upon a stick

A tattered coat upon a stick

Christopher Levenson

QUATTRO BOOKS

The publication of *A tattered coat upon a stick* has been generously
supported by the Canada Council for the Arts and the Ontario Arts Council.

Canada Council   Conseil des arts
for the Arts   du Canada

ONTARIO ARTS COUNCIL
CONSEIL DES ARTS DE L'ONTARIO
an Ontario government agency
un organisme du gouvernement de l'Ontario

Author's Photograph: Oonagh Berry
Cover image: Sigrid Albert
Cover design: Zile Liepins
Typography: Diane Mascherin
Editor: Allan Briesmaster

Library and Archives Canada Cataloguing in Publication

Levenson, Christopher, author
    A tattered coat upon a stick / Christopher Levenson.

Poems.
ISBN 978-1-988254-40-1 (softcover)

    I. Title.

PS8573.E945T38 2017   C811'.54   C2017-900880-3

Published by Quattro Books Inc.
Toronto
www.quattrobooks.ca

Printed in Canada

As always, for Oonagh

An aged man is but a paltry thing,
A tattered coat upon a stick, unless
Soul clap its hands and sing, and louder sing,
For every tatter in its mortal dress.

– W.B. Yeats, "Sailing to Byzantium"

CONTENTS

WEED

From the end of the war I remember them,
before cranes and pile drivers came to reconstruct
a taller and denser City, those derelict lots,
bomb sites left over from the Blitz, where every cranny
ran wild with willowherb, small shrubs and nettles,
seeded by birdlime or planted by the wind,
nature's graffiti on eroded brick.
Likewise our mongrel tongue:
no formal Versailles gardens, a topiarist's dream,
where every mini tree, perruqued and pruned back,
reflects its fellow's clarity and order.

English resisted schooling.
Wastrel, vagabond, it wandered the world, rubbed together
the small change of Anglo-Saxon, Norman French,
pedantic Renaissance Latin, tossed in thieves' argot,
smatterings picked up from skippers, rajahs, tycoons
in distant harbours (kow-tow, juggernaut,
imbroglio, schadenfreude, guru, safari, thug)
then shipped them home, a galleon's worth of words.
Yet this rough and ready crew now rules the roost,
profuse as purple loosestrife, everyone's favourite
second language, though still a homeless urchin,
butt of my homage, adaptive, endlessly fickle.

DANGLING MAN

Listening to words spun out
at a lunchtime poetry gig,
from the corner of my eye, I see
a man on a rope, no action hero,
hovering
by the walls of the building opposite,
as somewhere above
on the roof as he rappels
downwards from floor to floor
a creaking winch pays out
lengths of hawser, a bucket.

Poets and window cleaners
hone the same precarious skills,
practice a tricky balance
to make us see more clearly.

At Large

ANNIVERSARY, 2003

Strapped into Calvinist certainties, winter returns
to Overflakkee, Schouwen-Duiveland.
Despite causeways and dykes, fifty years later
the contours of sea and land continually
re-invent themselves, perspectives never stand still.
Greenhouses, church spires, barns, a line of poplars –
there's always something breaking up the horizon
into manageable lots. Today every farmhouse strains
with flags for the Queen's visit,
retracing her mother's steps when she waded in thigh boots
through the mud of flooded villages.

Beyond, in the open fields those memories
are embodied in water, long channels scooped out by the sea
near where the dykes broke. Otherwise
Bruinisse, Oude-Tonge and Oosterland
seem tranquil suburbia as though it had never happened.
With the polders clean, their furrows etched in snow,
all is in order again.

BERLIN REVISITED*

Few remnants litter the city I first saw
in the fall of '53. Even though, late September,
galaxies of fallen yellow leaves,
abandoned like *Judensterne*,
still clutter the sidewalks,
the whole-face transplant has taken.

The modern is back, high-rises make new
unambiguous statements:
former "degenerate" art is reinstated,
with a gallery for Emil Nolde, a museum
and a square named for Käthe Kollwitz
in the former East Sector,
where the nearby water tower,
one of the Nazis' first interrogation sites,
is simply a tourist landmark.
The Hauptbahnhof, like Piranesi's
imaginary prisons,
constructs a glass cascade
of interlocking sections.

I can no longer enter
the maze of the past:
peaceful houseboats along the Spree,
new street names, new statuary –
Karl Liebknecht's, Rosa Luxemburg's stony gaze –
and that huge underground memorial
put a whole new face upon
the Holocaust's headlong dark
that ended here.

* See Notes

AT THE WALL

In this part of Berlin
memorials everywhere
settle into the sidewalk,
a forest of brass names
not stars or celebrities:
constellations of loss
stir under my feet.
"Arrested in '42, murdered in Auschwitz"
or three decades later
"shot while climbing the Wall."
These silences converge.
Only a small step
from Gestapo to Stasi,
the same faces prevail.
Their losses unconsoled,
these neighbour citizens,
the mulch of history,
united at last in death.

SANS SOUCI*

Outside, a mini Versailles, a vast parterre,
vistas of empire, careless solitude.
Within the galleries, too much,
a rampant bewilderment of limbs
swimming in clouds, acres of surplus flesh,
bosom and belly, decorate the ceilings.
Amor and Psyche, Cupids sprawl everywhere,
over marble pillars, jasper walls
classical, biblical paraphernalia.

In picture frames gold-embossed,
three or four paintings high,
enough Watteau and Lancret to last a lifetime.
Their rococo blandishments lure aristocrats
to play at shepherd and shepherdess, refining
their postures towards the simple life.

Too busy frolicking in their make-believe,
they do not see Chardin's cook return to her kitchen
from market, laden with vegetables.

* See Notes

DATELINES
for Nelofer Pazira

These latest missionaries
instead of bibles carry
notepads, tape recorders,
the veil replaced at most
by a perfunctory headscarf
over their flak jackets.

Partnered only by
interpreters, cameramen,
they are brought in by jeep
or helicopter, left
alone in a no man's land
to disturb the violent dust
of Somalia, Afghanistan.

Though no one grants safe passage
through checkpoints, ambushes,
somehow these women can,
for all their western gear,
stare down Kalashnikovs
and probe behind the silence
of their veiled sisterhood,
divining, then tapping into
overlooked aquifers
of truth below the desert,
giving voice to the pain
of slums and settlements,
letting caged women speak,
allowing their screams to be heard.

To mortify our flesh
they are embedded like shrapnel
in the living corpse of empire.

FINDINGS

Out of season in a rented car, November,
I travel west, prospecting for later visits;
Lynmouth, Boscastle, Tintagel. Pacing around
high cliffs and windscaped headlands, hidden bays,
places I had not seen in fifty years,
I disinter the bones of my childhood's end.

In 1945 I was eleven when, with my little brother
Geoffrey suddenly dead, our depleted family
went camping in Devon and Cornwall and everything
started unravelling. I remember the rain
and our chilly absent-heartedness, but aside from Clovelly,
all rose-covered lintels and cream teas, it remains a blur.

Now, stirred by early morning, as I drive
the last flocks of mist are herded by the wind.
On the wide moors I relish this austere
spectral beauty in my own time – sheer barns, a skyline
distinct, uncluttered by greenery. I see for miles
pastures and woodland scathed by Atlantic gales.

Closer to hand on the rock face I decipher scrawls
of lichen blotted by moss. Revenant, how come,
after so long gone, attuned to a different pace,
I find myself again in these frugal villages
and stone market squares of an England living still?
What peace can I found in a country that might have been?

RENERNIG*
for Yvon and Val

Almost seven a.m., I stand
at the window, in hope of daylight
but scan only myself
framed in the still dark.
Outside on steep meadows mist
rises like chloroform
till at last the early sun
slowly rekindles the day,
brings to light every cornice,
picks out dormer windows,
pressing its random tribute
on kitchen garden, barnyard floor.
Now it sends warmest regards
to ancient cottage walls
bewildered with lavender.

Once again it is dusk:
here, deep in Brittany,
beyond the reach of phones
and, out of touch with everything
except for sunlight, leaves,
I still struggle to find my voice
in an all but forgotten father
tongue. Then catch my breath
as shadows slowly advance
into the trees, seize the flanks
of the nearest hillside, and watch
my friend's ancestral stone,
its inherited calm,
investing everything
with the absolution of silence.

* See Notes

FABRIC
for Kimsooja

As a child in a thatched hut
she scratched her first drawings
on the frost of interior walls.
Now woman, she has gathered
cast-offs from everywhere,
joined abandoned fabrics
by patient handiwork,
woven, soft to the touch,
sari and salwar kameez,
shards of cotton, silk, cashmere
until they are all –
turquoise, vermillion, ochre –
reborn into a bundle,
a burden taken up
by travellers, a yarn.

Jagged sunlight down
a Mumbai slum alley
re-ignites heaps
of beaten laundry, slapped
by dhobi wallahs into
the whole world's rainbow flags.

Gashes of colour reek
from the dank shanties;
in passing suburban trains
vivid faces explode
as tears or laughter
unfold to auras of light.

As the fabric of everyday
grows frayed, hangs by a thread,
we shall need many more
of such imaginings.

ONE YEAR AFTER

One year after the Japanese tsunami,
thousands of miles to the east
and shorn of all context
the ocean regurgitates its swag:
the detritus of nightmare
is beached on the BC coast –
a toxic cargo of toys,
a basketball, whole sheds,
a motorbike, a boat – everything
the sea could bear
to take upon itself.
Though nothing can reconstitute
those lives, this delirium
of abandoned goods, reduced
by wind and tide,
remains anonymous,
drifts here to bring home
to us, who want for nothing,
disaster's cornucopia.

Transcanada

LITTORAL

Here on the front lawn instead of a rusted '64 Chevy
a fishing smack lies beached
in the long grass between the tool shed
and the bleached timber of the shingled roof.

As if by some homing instinct
or a whale's radar gone awry,
boats have been thrust beyond
their usual coves and salt marshes, made
helpless amphibians.

And that man in the blue sweater staring out
from a dormer window into starless night over the bay,
is he some second Noah, in his salt bones aware
such craft may be needed soon?

AUBADE
Saint-Fabien-sur-Mer

Waking at dawn, a few yards from the beach
I watch the sprawl of seaweed slowly returning
from black to umber, ochre, green.
The rock pool's hidden silver, tarnished by night, is restored
to brilliance by the winds' asperity. But light it is
lends everything beauty, makes headlands emerge
from cloud drifts, and across the wide St. Lawrence
shadings of grey pick out that farther shore
till the landscape is again articulate.

DISTANCE
for George Amabile

All year long Winnipeg is primed
for winter: at street level, lockdown,
nothing happens to hold the eye,
nothing to tether the wind. A mile-long freight train
slides out of sight behind the totem high-rises
of Bank and Wheat Board, the spaces between
blocked in by vacant parallels, cool
anonymity. In gold we trust.

Not far from the newly opened
cathedral to Human Rights,
where I must concentrate
on Auschwitz, Armenia,
I am distracted by news nearer home:
a battered native woman's torso dredged
from the banks of the Red River,
one in over a thousand.

In the Manitoba Museum, a host of artefacts,
beadwork pouches, bison scapula
made into squash knives,
primitive masks of pain and apology,
from stains tattooed into our past,
safe behind plexiglass, now
the Métis are part of our heritage.

Down by The Forks the disappeared
are audible in the wind, in the blown grass.
Their memory wafts by in sweetgrass, tribal drums.
But if "words are medicine," for them
they come too late. "No woman is an island,
every woman a piece of the continent,
a part of the main," that ancient inland sea.

They are "not high on our radar."
After all, like the city's street plan,
it's a matter of distance, perspective. The women
are starting the long way home.

IN PRAISE OF FLAT COUNTRY

I who love mountains, the abrupt clamour
of space breaking loose
under my feet, rock angles, obstinate
gushing veins of wind picking at
tufts of high grass, the free fall
of water crashing
into far silence –
I who cherish all this
nevertheless find peace here
in the platitudes of landscape
exposed to noon heat and reeds
that embroider an indolent river,
greenhouses, kitchen gardens, close-cropped
hundred-acre fields, a seemingly bland
geometry. Surprised, I find within me
a soft spot for flat lands,
can welcome straight roads, the illusion
of safe community.
                    Sometimes the dramatic
overwhelms, sometimes I too need
to return to the plain, to submit
to more minute perspectives, making my everyday
among silos, cowsheds, barns, crammed to the rafters
with harvest and docile, breathing flanks. Lifelines
converge at, say, MacGregor's Corners, no-nonsense
wind-scoured remote places
with a general store and a gas pump, enough
to get me by, not always, but for now.

TRANSCANADA

Standing outside the prairie motel at the highway's edge,
I know I could never see it this way
without Colville and Lemieux. I have grown into
their sense of emptiness, stillness. Unconsciously I hear
birdcries from wetlands, sense overbearing horizons,
the road going on towards nightfall,
and nothing to be seen on either side
until, tomorrow, the mountains.
Roadsides cannot convey the distances
within the mind, the wind wrestling the grass,
endless freight trains howling between
Edmonton, Regina, Thunder Bay.

This country I can never get enough of:
white settlements of snow, between times the underlying
brown earth asserting its primacy,
that first world, how
to take it all in, include
also what does not fit, the random, how to pass by
unnecessary structures. No need for speech.
This is something the eye can embrace, the ear attend to –
something our veneer of civility
would like to forget predates this maze
of high tension wires, oil pipelines, tailings ponds
debouching into lakes, infrastructure, underpinnings
grown haphazardly over two centuries.

PATTERNS

Thirty thousand feet below
a scattering of cloud
and then Saskatchewan
wrinkled with streams,
tiny lakes and coulees
breaking up the tawny ground.

I am still taken by
landscape's patterning,
its slow-motion history,
the way that over time
in glacial synthesis
valleys evolve, rivers
scour or smooth down
recalcitrant outcrops, erasing,
soothing all into compliance,
a vast static inland sea.

Now, only minutes later
over the foothills, change:
striations everywhere,
surfaces pucker up, fracture,
mountainsides mossed with shadow,
scant vestiges of snow
dazzle below the peaks.
Bright sun makes it hard to know
where water ends, shade begins.

From this height it is easy
to overlook the chaos
pioneers left behind
as, centuries past, they struck out
through forest and canyon,
staked claims on a countryside
not theirs to own, built stockades,
settlements. All that remains
ghost towns, husks, carrion. Nothing
is permanently civilized.
The sun, wind, rock
hold sway eternally.

FLYING TO KAMLOOPS

Sparse lances of sunlight
on the early mountainsides
sparingly pick out,
illuminate
a golden stand of trees
against the evergreen.
There rivers infiltrate
hinterlands barely broached
by roads, still undisturbed
outcrops of the primitive
glacial residues,
turquoise lakes collecting
below the peaks. Remnants of snow
flash a salute as the plane
banks down and battlements
of scarp reel back till again
green yields to tumbleweed, desert brown,
broad valleys of everyday.

GETTING TO KNOW YOU

For my wife, a native of Dublin, it was "the wrong ocean."
All the same, sea-smells, kelp, foghorns, the whole bit
that we both had between our teeth as kids, even
the fragrance of rain, is restored, lends us new life:
for the first time since the 60s in Bristol I wake to ships' horns.
Little by little the city reveals itself
in short-cuts, hidden neighbourhoods uncovered.
So I learn to cherish and praise
places on earlier visits I hardly noticed:
that communal garden on Cypress
where long before my time here, train tracks ran,
and now great gushers of forsythia daze the eyes.
How many winters will pass before I tire
of these abrupt vistas of the coastal mountains,
the sea heaving below me, leaving me stunned
at my strange belonging here?

Towards evening across from Yaletown high-rises make
a bright mosaic of our night sky, project
glacial indifference, galaxies
of penthouse and balcony thrust upwards
for a better view of the next apartment's
daze of bright windows set against velvet,
studs on a screen. Their flex and interflow
creates an electric tapestry, cascading surfaces,
an urban borealis. At every level
glass obelisks, sliced and dissected,
like a shaken kaleidoscope, collapse
into False Creek, their grids coalescing in darkness.

As I watch, flash floods of traffic
carouse down arteries, converge onto bridges
at Burrard, Granville, Cambie, headlights, taillights in spate,
like red and white corpuscles. Cars and trucks ricochet
across divided highways, then suddenly sheer off,
trajectories of light racing beyond
the Second Narrows Bridge and Burnaby Mountain
into remotest suburbia. The light plasma pulsates
across highways, grows intermittent, fading

into hushed farmland, pasture, market gardens.
As countryside takes over, harvests the darkness,
developers' dreams of endless commuter suburbs,
settlements on the edge, are warehoused, put on hold.

So, slowly in what is becoming my home I find my way
by car, by bus, by SkyTrain, by trial and error,
stitch my own patchwork quilt of the city
till I finally know it almost by heart and can often
set my bearings by church spire, apartment block
as they emerge like marker buoys
on a sea of green trees now shedding, turning to winter.
I watch as in quicksilver feints of light, the city secretes
mystery or yields to morning's candour,
with the skyline open to view, *tabula rasa*
for imagination to dwell in.

This city grows on me, like moss or lichen:
within five years I have acquired a patina.

DEFINING MOMENTS

Strange how those lights strung out
on the mountain peak ski slope
have come to define the morning.
The view from my bedroom window
tells me at once if the day's set to be fair,
for now at least, until
the wind changes its mind, foreshadows
some other shape in the unforeseen
chloroform clouds that clamp down
on the distant hillside.

It's a start at least. Later the landscape
is free to flesh out with colours
the shale light coming in,
flooding all creeks and inlets,
exposing the angles of boatyards,
slipways, travelling cranes,
and submerging the darkness.

At the call of the phoebe
the neighbourhood slowly awakes.

FIRST LIGHT

Grasp at the morning;
it slips through your fingers, has vanished
like mist on the mountains.
Like aspen, like willow,
before you can properly savour
the freshness of meadows and valleys
it is already saying
farewell.

AS MISTS UNWIND ...

As mists unwind from the valleys,
drifting over us, filtering through
first hasty drafts of morning,
in maroon and black the tankers,
riding at anchor out beyond English Bay,
impose their local colour,
while I wait for the glass, steel mountains
of downtown to solidify.

FLARE-UP

For a few seconds only
on clear winter mornings, the sun
gold-washes corporate slabs,
those bullion citadels, emblazons
with flashpoints of stark colour
the windows of office blocks,
outlines cranes that hover
over the skeletons
of half-finished buildings
still crowned with scaffolding.

EARLY SPRING, KITS POINT

From so many tongues of leaf
such tentative
utterance, all dusty muted pink,
lilac, delicate off-white.
Like veils of false modesty
blossoms drizzle past
veranda and alleyway.

But how can these intricate
nuances, hesitations
ever appease my hunger for
India's stark purple, crimson?
Even magnolias'
magnificent candelabra
pale, cannot satisfy.
Let the hibiscus flare,
fire up those rhododendrons!

INFILL

Like macro-dental therapists,
backhoes and cranes replace
mere shacks with clean, new implants,
concrete and glass supplant
the peeling wood veneer.
Among the laid-back villas,
trappings of home make way
for the picture-perfect upstart.
Straight and narrow, it knows its place,
signed, sealed, and delivered
on time and under budget
to spruce new owners.
Eventually it will
acquire a few saving graces,
a patina, a lived-in look.
For now all it needs to do
is fit in, interlock.

DRIVING NORTH ALONG CLARK

Beyond the junction with Hastings
dockyard cranes suddenly
elate me as no tourist mecca could.
At all hours tractor-trailers make for
this haven of harsh yellow,
the massive steel rhetoric
of wharves and gantries,
whose stark vertical clamour
seems to frame the green
surrounding mountains
in welcoming counterpoint.

IN THE PUBLIC LIBRARY
for John Donlan

At ten a.m. sharp they rush in:
Shelter! Salvation!
The man on the street can find here
a place to retire from the world,
a safe house, warm
hideout without the prayers.

Browsing these catacombs,
eyeing the stacked tabloids
as possible blankets,
they learn to share their silence
with other denizens:
serious scholars addicted
to mediaeval arcana,
hermits surviving on
a few footnotes per day,
or a Karl Marx wannabe
picking at his beard, his nose,
his filing cards,

and of course school kids
researching, say, Homer's oral
tradition on the internet.
Yet despite the stark cubicles
of light, this is no skeleton:
at closing time they emerge
note-perfect, stifling yawns,
as from a living body.

BEACH

Tidings, a mesh of evanescent
water straddling the sand,
murkily flexible:
long fingerings of foam explore
broken crab shells, driftwood, detritus,
rake the shore clean,
then swiftly retreat, coalesce
once more with the waves' surface,
the roar, the sudden onrush.

BIRD SANCTUARY

At the onset of winter, beyond the airport, we drove
to the delta's furthest outreach, trudged past sloughs
babelled with ducks and seafowl, climbed an iron tower
skeined with frost to scan November marshes.
Thousands of snow geese were gathered among the reeds,
marshalled by unseen commands, to form elsewhere
in kinder climates some vast diaspora.
At last their steady wingbeat bludgeons the air,
a blizzard of birds takes off, whirrs,
wheels into the low horizon.

OUR PROFANE SAVIOURS

Somewhere downtown, the spars
of a misshapen cross
are outlined in neon. All night,
beyond English Bay, False Creek,
from my bedroom window
I can make it out, a developer's
crane. These profane saviours
have taken over the skyline.
Like Rio's Christ the Redeemer,
the crane extends its arms
in steady aspiration, bids
for untold future wealth
in the hereafter. Even at night
it illuminates the darkness.

ONSET

The mountain steeps in
pine solitudes. I question
the waterfall's lament.
Enough to know clouds already
possess the high valleys,
snow's urgent whisperings
drift to our threshold.
The fields lie fallow,
silence will ensue.

VICTORIA, BC

In this mild, white city,
an early trading post
en route to Yukon and Klondike
has been pushed aside to make way
for motorized wheelchairs.

Veterans and widows
take cover from the sun
which will soon like broadloom soothe
plaid skirts and tinted hair
to permanent repose.

The vistas of distant mountains
each corner here brings to light
are framed by flowering shrubs,
an uneasy paradise
of crimson, magenta, purple.

This city of sleek lawns
in whose receptive soil
everything flourishes
is surrounded by sea
that is reticent, knows its place.

AT THE PACIFIC RIM

Ocean and wind together
scour the forested shore,
to gouge out granite headlands,
sculpting fossil and bone
into prehistory.
We could stand here all day
just gazing at the horizon,
interpreting surfaces
or the wilderness of sky
blazoned with contrails.

Those planes go the distance,
to Tokyo, Sydney, Beijing
oblivious to the breakers'
probing, relentless thrust
into rockpools, disturbing

relics of past storms.
Now, having come so far,
we savour the edge: maybe,
ageing, we need no more
than wave surge, sharp tangle of pine.

Preserves

MACAW

in memoriam P.K. Page

Fitting that in Brazil
you had a pet macaw,
for such an alert
brilliantly mocking
creature becomes you:

Fine feathers, a finer
intellect, and a bright,
sharply observing eye.
They too live long
and have long memories.
Their purple and gold
emblazons the foliage,
they communicate
exactly.

So, incandescent, you
fly up, to guide us through,
ablaze with words,
inquisitive, elegant.
How could we not believe
you would be there forever?

But now the bird has flown.

FOR A FRIEND

in memoriam Philip Hobsbaum

Squat in your armchair, abrupt, combustible,
you sit like a latter-day Dr. Johnson surrounded by props:
bottle-glass spectacles against astigmatism,
at your side walking stick
like an extra wagging finger to prod your points home.
But chortling for all that. I can still hear you
expostulate, "insist" on some disputed reading.

Obstreperous patriarch,
what call did you have to become my older brother,
critical bludgeoner, impresario ("I made you, Levenson,"
you once said). Pushy, pint-sized Jehovah! Like any atheist
I waste too much breath blaspheming, denying you,
forgetting the good you did for me and others.
Obtuse, rotund, hospitable – you still, dammit, bulk too large.
I am not done with you yet.

INTRUDERS
for Roger and Joy

Out of the tacit woods
leaves part and soundlessly
a mother fox and her cub
encroach upon our squares
of domesticated light.

We who invaded their
habitat merely watch,
withholding all sound
as they approach to where
Roger, my friend,
and miniature Saint Francis,
has stealthily left out food
on the lawn for squirrels, foxes.

PILOT LIGHT
for Anthony

Once learnt, who can forget
how to swim, ski, ride a bike?
Even decades later an unused,
forgotten language surfaces,
a few words, a new beginning.
So with our friendship:
its constant pilot light
over time, over distances,
holds warmth in readiness.

KRUSKA VODA
for Ernst Poser

The first time, near Belgrade fifty years ago
it was homemade, by a painter who lived on the Danube
in a ramshackle houseboat studio and was the smoothest
liquor I ever tasted. Since then nothing has matched it.
Ernest, you re-introduced me
to that astringent sweetness, your words distilling
long buried memories. Too soon your death
has branded me, sealed in that flavour.

ONE MAN IN HIS TIME

in memoriam Charles Haines

Though you are gone almost a year now, your name
still graces your office door and from time to time
letters alight in your pigeon hole, like the doves of peace
you welcomed aboard your ark.

A *rara avis* yourself, often in transit alone
and to distant places – New Zealand, Russia, the Falklands –
you never went so far you forgot to send cards
to colleagues, or letters to the *Citizen*.

Not just a character actor, aged Hotspur
and Falstaff rolled into one, you took on many parts,
swashbuckled, had no time for academic
pettiness, lambasted hypocrites, pedants.

First Michael, then Jim, then you – it is getting tedious
lamenting these early deaths, and always the ones I was
most at ease talking to. But above all your students mourn you
and the hallways still echo to your blustering laughter.

STAGE SET
for Leah and Lynx

After tea and homemade cookies
you unfold blueprints, the bare bones
of the apartment you intend to share.
Gingerly in winter half-light we explore
your future habitat. Naked bulbs dangle
from outlets where the future ceiling will be.
The cement floor
is booby-trapped with electric wiring, tools
of joiners, plasterers, carpenters. The drywall
is still two weeks away.
But you let us eavesdrop on your dream
as you wait in the wings, secure but apprehensive,
for a new home to emerge
from the dust of renovation.
You cannot know
what you are moving into.

"LIFE'S TOO SHORT!"
for Imtiaz Dharker

"We can't keep meeting like this," breathlessly
at the last minute in hotel lobbies, exchanging
views and books, jotting down e-mail addresses
and constantly "looking forward,"
while outside the airport taxi's throbbing,
to more leisurely conversations,
with everything on hold, on stand-by.

Quaysides, departure lounges: diary entries
compact like garbage, our memories are bribed
by keepsakes, empty calories
while the real presence of a friend –
scent, handbag, veiled smile, a sleeve's warm pressure –
escapes through Security like the backyard flash
of a cardinal vanishing into nearby woods
as our bulging hopes still circle
unclaimed on the carousel.

LONG DISTANCE
for Gieve

At all hours I call you, to
restore contact. Behind the ringing tone,
porous, a mesh of voices
in tongues I cannot make out – Marathi? Gujarati?
in a city I have twice visited. How in this Babel
will I get through?

Who knows what's happening there? Newscasts
don't tell the whole story. Maybe,
since you last wrote, private disasters.
I calculate, half a world away,
ten and a half time zones, how you must be
asleep or, already in your tomorrow,
leaving for work, relaxing after a meal.
I hoped I had found a friend
for the long haul. Tell me it is so.
Yet, till we meet face to face,
we can never be in sync,
our long-distance voices like beggars
working the night.

A SHELL

in memoriam Helene Rosenthal

The ocean that scoured you once
is grown mere whisper; little enough remains
of that creative fury. Smiling and elegant
in the old way, you are securely lodged here,
random as driftwood, far from the tide's reach.
You have been
dispossessed, friendships pass
slowly across the horizon.
Your hazy blue eyes, kindly oblivious, fix
on distant beaches, sands
you can no longer tread.

PRESERVES
for Carol Shields

Essences of summer, early fall:
the plucked fruit, peeled and cut and slowly melding,
squeezed reluctant juices into a jar.
The past resolves into sunlit conversations
grouped round a kitchen table, a walk on the lawn,
or, recovering from public honours, your quick laughter
restoring balance. For each of us something
to take away, later recall
with sad affection that has now nowhere to go.
Already we taste your absence but maybe
mulberry, redcurrant, damson, tamarind,
fermenting, can fortify
this piquancy of loss.
At least, communing with your books,
we can partake of you, hope to preserve
during our own lifetimes
the recipe of yourself.

Counterpoint:
for Johannes Brahms

Allegro

That fall, my first job, teaching high school
in the east of Holland after a colleague sold me
my first LPs, yours was the chamber music
that drifted to me like woodsmoke across the meadows,
a music of longing restrained,
intransigent as stone. I felt I had always known
where you were coming from: like a distant shower
slanting across the horizon I have unconsciously
grown into it, like an inheritance.
                                    Much later I learnt about
your childhood home in Hamburg, though nothing remains
of your birthplace: in the last war, firestorms cauterised
your childhood habitat. One generation away
from open country, as a teen you were drawn to folksong,
compiled your own catalogues.
With mentors, teachers, friends predicting greatness
and the first departure from family, on tour with Joachim,
then staying with the Schumanns, you became itinerant.
Though a dutiful, loving son, in vain your mother
tried to lure you back at Christmas, promising eggnog, Marsala,
or sent you knitted socks. You were seldom at home.
Instead from en route, "in great haste" –
"I don't write letters, I answer them" –
you scribbled postcard regrets for non-attendance,
and lodged with friends in Berlin, Prague, Baden-Baden.
So often in transit, you became
a virtuoso of Baedekers, railway schedules.
With so much left to discover,
between the lines, in station waiting rooms,
you never contracted a full-blown case of letters.

Though denied the longed-for post in Hamburg, you could not
                                                    let go,
and yet, as you said to Clara, after the second rebuff,
with the road not taken to domesticity,

"One wants to have ties and a livelihood
that makes a life into a life and one is afraid
of loneliness. Activity in lively union with others
and lively social relations, family happiness —
what human being
doesn't feel a longing for that?"
                                    Slowly, however,
Vienna enveloped you and when the call finally came
you were too settled with friends and your lakeside summers
to move again. Though even then, with at last a fixed address,
your travelling trunk and valises stood under the window,
packed, ready for instant use.

Adagio

So much subjunctive, autumnal — hopes, wishes, desires.
As the mist, lifting
above the harbour, halfway down the mountain
hints at tentative brightness, resolves
in a resurgence of shapes — church spires and houses —
slowly re-emerging as if from a dream,
so you, leaving home, created a tentative balance.

Hermann Levi saw in you
"the image of a pure artist and man,"
yet one who could with Agatha abandon
the certain hope of marriage and family,
preferring a chosen solitude, continuity
through art alone.

In Clara Schumann you found early
a kindred spirit, a love (as she said
"I love him as a son, so tenderly")
that interwove both your lives.
Though constant, sustainable,
for you it was never enough.
No one outside could sense
how much you shared.

Four decades long your melodies intertwined
with hers, your first auditor.
With her interests at heart, in mind, in memory,
she flowed into waiting scores,
as hidden sustenance, aquifer.
When she lay dying
you came with your Four Serious Songs,
as funeral offering, telling her daughter, Marie,
"Those eyes when they finally close will close
so much for me." Indeed
the mists came down once more:
after such loss less than a year remained.

Scherzo

For me you are both twin and distorting mirror.
Though you scorned formal evening wear,
preferring to wander around without collar and tie,
for some big occasions you grumpily dressed up
like one of the seven dwarfs,
then enjoyed it after all.

Trickster and acrobat, liking banter and practical jokes
with Liesl and Henry, you were fifteen times called upon
to be a godfather, and always a hit with children:
giving Widmann's little daughter piggyback rides
through the streets of Zurich and at times caught,
caught up in snowball fights.
Nor with your own first publications,
could you get used to seeing
"these children of nature dressed so respectably."

Saturated with kindness
towards children and animals,
you were at ease with the local peasantry,
who saw you as one of their own.
On holiday, always an early riser,
a German Triton blowing the French horn,
you skinny-dipped in the mountain lake
when no one else was around.

Likewise, you fed the stove with letters,
covered the tracks of your hidden kindnesses.
Yet what I admire in you most
amongst the laughter in even the lightest song,
trace elements of grief encroaching on
slow-motion darknesses.

Allegro
"Denn alles Fleisch es ist wie Gras"
(For all flesh is like grass)

Music unseals the secret labyrinths
where hopes and fears lie hidden, fugitive,
and releases the sea within
to heal the silent and the dispossessed.
After your mother's death and the German Requiem,
you gathered grass by the sheaf, to store, and restore
to blend with memories and foreshadowings.

Yet despite the "eternal note of sadness"
in Vienna you were at ease.
Though honours came, even Cambridge's offered
Doctorate could not tempt you
into a Channel crossing. You remained yourself,
acknowledged master, settled at last among
admiring friends, mindful of family,
secretly generous to those in need.
No lover of metronomes,
disdainful of cliques and flattery,
you remained yourself, somehow balancing
lament and jubilation,
solitude with the need for company,
a *Stammtisch* at the Roten Igel.

Then, after too long a break
through the Double Concerto,
you made your peace with Joachim,
restoring harmony, recommended Dvořák
to your own publisher (you wrote to Simrock
"You know I do not lightly recommend"),
admiring Verdi, who like you was a child of the people,
had known early hardship, self-taught, little time for theory.

In your last years hearing Richard Mühlfeld play
the clarinet entranced you out of retirement
into a final surge of enthusiasm,
lured you into new tones, sadness and gaiety
lovingly intertwined.
                              As I grow older
your clarity endures, and I love hearing afresh
those disembodied voices
on my pacific shore, and am at peace.

The Home Stretch

AT THE DENTIST'S

In this bleak sanctuary,
where Venetian blinds
fillet daylight into
manageable slices
and screen out the passersby,
I present myself for cleaning.

The reclining chair, equipped
with all the latest high-tech
aerodynamic steel
becomes my confessional –
When did you last floss? –
though here instead of plainchant
piped music surrounds me.

As I lie inert, mouth gaping,
a gowned priest attends.
Acolytes, sterile handmaidens,
pass him his instruments,
with which to probe soft tissue,
seek out my obdurate pockets
of decay. Remorse of conscience
bites me again. I wince and take
a Dixie cup to absolve, swill away
gargoyle impurities.
Gifted with an immaculate
plastic-encased toothbrush
to work at my backslidings,
I do my penance, promise
a more hygienic future.

Then numbly I am dismissed
into the world again.

AQUAFIT

Some antique ritual:
for an hour in the enormous sunlit pool
I am the anonymous token male
among a score of large elderly ladies
swaying like lily pads
to the pounding disco beat.
All eyes are fixed ahead on the instructor,
whose arms and legs, lithe as a Hindu goddess,
are showing us what to do.
Like trainee astronauts
we follow her in slow motion,
shedding our pounds, toning our muscles,
relishing weightlessness.

AT SEA
for Niall

Behind you on shore, postponed,
the doldrums of family. Here
on the catamaran you can be
yourself, alone
struggling against the bluster,
the big wind's embrace, fifteen-foot waves
that summon every muscle as you strain
to keep sails taut, steady the boat.
There is no letup, no time now
to dive into the self, your mind
has set its course, is blank
of all ambivalence.
A few clear landmarks
and all the rest is physical,
mastery, brute survival,
whereas at home charts,
sextant, compass, are useless.
Whatever they throw at you,
the seas are easier.

TREMORS

A few months before Hiroshima
my nuclear family
exploded. Now only photographs
remind me of my brother
who died March '45
on his eighth birthday.
The fall-out lasted decades.

No seismograph can trace
how deep in the earth's core
the shock of that death went,
nor for how long
tremors persisted. Too soon
I realized the earth
was inherently unstable.

THE WATCH

What shall I do with this watch my father gave me,
what, fifty years ago? I have lost count.
Unlike the Rolex he wore until his death,
which I inherited, it was modestly accurate. If it can't be fixed
I'll buy a new one soon. And yet my wrist without it
still feels naked: so long handcuffed to time
I cannot make out my unaccustomed freedom.

I have passed on the Rolex to my son,
the one who has time for me.
It's almost my only heirloom, water-resistant
(as I am not) but by now like me in a world
of cellphones, iPods, YouTubes, mere antique.
Self-winding in response to the body's movements,
the ticker tells minutes and hours, its luminous face
no longer glows in the dark, its hands
only mark time. For me time hangs on my hands
like Spanish moss. I feel the need to unwind.

IN THE BUS

Aural voyeur despite myself, I am trapped
in the Babel of half a dozen lives'
ambient solitudes. It's like
a telephone exchange: everyone young
groping in their jeans or purses for
instant technology, preoccupied
with faraway voices, music.
                                        Up at the front
an old drunk, disconnected but jolted awake
by someone's ring tone, trots out his monologue
to fellow passengers, but no one's listening.

PROFESSIONALS

Specialists for every part, these doctors
explore niche markets of knowledge,
staking out claims on our bodies,
here an eye, there an esophagus.

Like Aztec sacrifices we are delivered
on time to their machines,
subjected to X-rays, MRIs, ultrasound
and patiently await their diagnosis.

Only thus can these masked high priests
of medicine document
degeneration, natural decay.
Over-exposed, we shrink.

Are we more than serviced lots,
areas of expertise? As consoles
of instruments take our measure
it is hard not to wonder if
in their daily lives they too
are mere blundering amateurs.

SWEET!

"Sweet!" The approval, delight
of teenagers, love's cravings satisfied.

Where once I was seduced
by honeycomb, baklava,
my now jaded tongue recoils
from excessive sweetness. Cured
of a thousand velvet addictions,
apprentice curmudgeon, sourpuss,
I scrutinize jams at the supermarket,
begrudge, try in vain to strain out
each gram of glucose.

The older I get the more
I demand stronger tastes –
lime, ginger, tamarind,
the tang of spices.
Sipping Campari neat,
I am at pains to test
its lingering bitterness.

GLOSSIES

Toro, Novo, GQ: abandoned newborns,
they arrive on my doorstep, swaddled
in the *Globe and Mail*, displaying the best
in print media production values – a surge of fast
supercharged sports cars, twinned with a flash
of leg, slit skirts and plunging necklines, figureheads
to drape the hood, trophies, arm candy. Not
a member of this gated community, I'm willy-nilly
voyeur, peeping tom at the soft porn of wealth:
the girls all sensual pout, a come-on look
from eyes half-turned away; a centrefold
for Armani suits, Bulgari diamonds, Hugo Boss,
with backdrops of Bond Street or the Champs-Élysées;
the young men – macho strut, sullen command –
scowl their desire. Through lethal, nonchalant
half-shaded eyes, they're intent
on making a killing, holding their own
in a bull market so they can swirl away
their languid playmates to Caribbean resorts
where suites start at a thousand a night.
Unlike the newsprint that shows me ruined
Lebanon, Darfur's anorexia,
these model lives exist on coated stock
that cannot be recycled.

FLOWER SHOW

While the dahlias and orchids look flustered,
applying last minute dabs
of colour, the gladioli
are virginally sheathed
for every eventuality
(but mostly funerals).
Under the judges' eyes
all's florid acquiescence:
these are society flowers,
suave, on the their best behaviour
at formal occasions
but lost outside their kempt gardens.

In such august company
sunflowers hang their heads
drowsily, or in shame;
even the lilies listlessly
recline in dust.

Soon I grow bored
with so much voluptuousness,
such plumped and overbearing
display. I dream of distant hedgerows,
where vetch and columbine,
wild poppies and black-eyed susans
proliferate unprized. I long
for thrift and scabious
that started from scratch,
grew up tough on salt flats
any old how, eked out a life
anywhere wind or birdlime
jettisoned them. They
never last long indoors
but make for good company
and in passing reveal
how to survive.

PEOPLE AT AN EXHIBITION

adopt all kinds of poses
that echo or are mocked by
Matisse, Picasso, Cézanne
as they bend over backwards
to understand
this outrage of colour.
Absentminded Saint Joans,
they are plugged in to voices
intoning on audio tapes
till the galleries jingle
with bird-like twitterings.

Even without such aids
they know which canvasses
deserve the longest stare.
Adjusting their postures,
gesturing, nodding,
they prove themselves
the perfect models.
In every room you can find
Manets or Modiglianis
but more suitably dressed
and none reclining nude.
Having paid an arm and a leg,
to enter, they now intend
to get their money's worth.

JOINING THE JEWISH FOLK CHOIR

It seemed a simple thing,
choosing a choir, a matter
of taste, styles of singing
closer to my desire
for ancient melodies
renewed in our own day,
intricacies of sound.

I was not looking for
a new community.
How come then I founder
so late in life, take on
another's history,
burdens not my own
or only at two removes,
as a ship, running aground,
lists, takes on water.

As I struggle through Yiddish, Ladino,
is it the music alone
I have grown to love?
Is it klezmer, Sephardic song,
fiddle, flute, clarinet,
that induce such a sense of belonging?
Or beneath the desert does
some Jewish aquifer
link me to broken pasts and irrigate my present?
Have I unwittingly
become a citizen?

SCAVENGERS

I admire those who make do
with what they can save or recycle,
not just the down-and-outs
ransacking back-alley trash cans,
to stuff their supermarket carts
and salvage empties for cash.

All hoarders, we are hard-wired
to retain most of what hurt us, seize on
stale-dated promises, scraps of false praise,
bitter words of farewell, trotting them out
at the height of an argument,
regretting it instantly.
Indiscriminate memory attracts
iron filings of malice, motives
forgotten or misconstrued.

Happy the Alzheimer's victims living beyond
their means of consistent recall
in the disconnected moment! For now
they have all they need, picking over
a lifetime's memories. We too like seagulls circle,
keen-eyed, waiting to swoop
on fragments of leftover life that might come in handy.

THRIFT STORE

Only slightly less chaotic than the city dump, but nirvana
for those who believe in luck or barely subsist
in a friendless, new environment with no Welcome Wagon to turn to,
here everything a depleted purse could desire, and more, far more,
from ancient Harris Tweed jackets to debutante gowns, is on display.

We scavenge the bins' cornucopia, hoping to find,
finger old lockets, jewels, probably paste,
but somebody's cherished trinkets once, teddy bears, toys,
a pink plastic barrette, an oil painting with deer,
or an adored china doll, likewise forsaken and gazing
with wide eyes at its comedown in the world.

And then the books, dog-eared, abandoned, adorned
with coffee stains and florid inscriptions or neat
marginal comments: Victorian sermons, memoirs, romance,
all that the literate heart could fancy blooming among, even photo
                                                        albums,
complete with sepia christenings, glossy weddings.

Who could have known how their lives would one day turn out,
resigned to this dingy chaos? But everything not given away or willed
to a favourite niece or grandchild ends here in limbo
for others to pick over. Accept the way of the world,
make yourself at home in oblivion.

QUILTS
for Martin Meissner

After the First World War
frayed remnants, odds and ends
of vanished empires
were hastily stitched together
into a makeshift pattern,
patches eked out
with threadbare promises.
Now after the Second,
we love to claim
we are whole cloth,
all one human fabric,
but at how many removes?
Nowhere's home anymore,
we are all emigres, vagrants.
Such careful embroidery
went to their fashioning,
textures, surfaces
that generations
lovingly embraced
on once familiar bodies!
Lost in new designs
we cannot recognize
our selves.
I scavenge these panels
for memories of countries
I once passed through,
each now in a different colour,
a different font, like ransom notes
to be pieced together, untraceable.
How can bright fragments in time
give the cover and warmth of home
to refugees sleeping rough?

COMPLICITY

Good Quaker that she was, my mother grew troubled
that her Building Society made her money
that she had never worked for. How we are taken in
by the logos of rugged pioneer firms,
trusted family names, as if we were buying into
a tradition! Yet when I case my larder –
Marmite, Becel, Maille mustard and Lipton's soups –
Unilever owns them all: everywhere multinationals
co-opt dreams of fair trade, corner the market
on olive oil, frozen cod. Nothing is what it seems.

Like sumac roots, ownership gropes underground,
seeps like tailings into my coffee cup.
By proxy we are all slavers –
exporting asbestos, adorning our heads with blood diamonds,
allowing Mexican farmhands to stake their lives
at minimum wage, because we can look away,
because my pension depends on it.
The glossy annual reports I discard unread:
I prefer not to know
how my assets metastasize.

Happy-face capitalism institutionalizes
greed, outsources conscience
where it will do no harm to the profit margin.
My few square feet of oil sands leech into my bloodstream.
At most I find room to stash my complicity
behind small-scale ironies, mental reservations.
Barcodes infest my mental DNA.
Which of us can afford to be innocent?

DISCONNECT

Thirty years back they built a dock, an idyllic log home, laid out
a flower garden busy with hummingbirds.
Self-sufficient in semi-retirement (only half an hour
by floatplane from the city), our hosts, a power couple,
are immune to the business routine, though still
connected by iPad, cellphone, never out of the loop.
As our son's friends, they can afford to be kind,
make us welcome as weekend visitors new to their island.

While crabs, locally caught, are dressed and boiled for dinner
we listen in to other guests' chat about yachts, the weather,
motorbikes, ferry schedules, real estate prices.
Not once did we cross the line into politics.
In return they ply us with drinks and their opinions
on the need for new tanker terminals, logging rights
but ask us no questions. Our green subversive views
are stifled in politeness. Over aperitifs
we hedge our silences, play with their Labradoodle.

It is past midsummer now. On this island
they choose not to observe the darkness advancing.

TECHNO-LOVERS

Even up at the cottage they cannot keep their hands off
each other's BlackBerrys, iPhones.
Down at the dock they are constantly fingering, checking
the markets, the girlfriend, the office,
afraid they might, God forbid, for even a second
find themselves off the grid and feel compelled
to gaze at boring water, monotonous trees
or hear the tweeting of birds, be aware of the loon.

Scherzo

LOVE AMONG THE TOMES

Explore me between the covers,
gently press back my spine:
though I've had other book lovers
for a month you'll be only mine.

Linen-bound, paperback, boxed –
what matters is what's inside.
Though my corners are slightly foxed,
as you see I have nothing to hide.

Seeking knowledge or release?
Just open me where you will,
linger over my frontispiece,
praise my twelve-point Baskerville,

and your darkest fear, your dearest wish
I'll conjure up all by myself
through card catalogue and microfiche.
Just don't leave me on the shelf!

So deface my purple passages,
underline me in felt pen,
annotate my anatomy,
take me out again and again.

But though I fulfill your fantasy,
I can never belong to you,
and you handled me so roughly,
now I'm two months overdue.

RUMINATIONS AT THE MANGER

Nobody asked us what we felt about it,
whether we minded abandoning our straw
for a couple of nights and having strangers trample
across the byre, invading our privacy
and leaving my best friend, Naomi the cow,
ten hours unmilked, not to mention my hooves sore
from standing so long. No, we were herded
– as you can see in the paintings – and made to gaze down
at the tiny haloed intruder, watching it suckle
at Mary's breast. We seem to be kneeling in worship
along with the kings and all their entourage.
And what did we get for it? Not even an extra carrot!
That kind of meekness may be OK for sheep,
those humble, fuzzy boulders dotting the hillside:
they'd follow any crook. But it's not what I'd call faith.
Simplemindedness, more like. Give me a break!
Anyway, now we're the poster animals, walk-on parts
for humility and gentle adoration,
mere docile, feel-good Christmas furniture.
But does that mean we no longer have to pull ploughs
or get harnessed in traps? Not a bit of it:
animal liberation theology
is still a long way off. Well, I'm done with rejoicing,
put out to pasture now, but I'm not your average
Middle-Eastern donkey. I think I might emigrate
to India where I hear even elephants
and monkeys can be gods.

A DOG'S LIFE

Here in Kits Point it's hard not to become
unwittingly a connoisseur of dogs:
at every corner a poodle or poodle mix
is leading its master up the garden path;
retrievers lie in wait for hours outside
the coffee shop; with angst-filled Kafkaesque eyes
a couple of dachshunds decode the fire hydrant's
cryptography; all regal benevolence,
mastiffs bear down on us; springer spaniels,
tails working like metronomes, strain at the leash
to sniff or be sniffed; and at every curbside
floppy puppies are walking four ways at once.
As well as the clinics and shops for pedicures, dog toys,
they even have their own beach, a very heaven
to run and swim in, and no stick too heavy
to rescue from the waves and wrestle ashore.

On the way home their well-trained owners carry
their gross domestic product in plastic bags
to glut the safe deposits of garbage bins.
Truly, Man is a dog's best friend.

VINTAGES

The only chateau I have ever stayed in –
three weeks one summer – was a fortress dating back
to the thirteenth century. Its keep and walls
lorded it over the village, its formal gardens
grew rampant with lavender. Though Marie, the chatelaine,
made appliqué tapestries as a sideline, her main joy
was collecting Parisian artists, playing *grande dame*
to her little colony of painters, poets, composers.

She showed us her "caves;" like VIPs Ulla and I
inspected the rows of bats, an honour guard
clamped to the barrel-vault ceiling. We admired
the passion that went into the making of wine.

Later we sampled a glass or two: smoky-purplish, a fume
straight from the earth. Maybe not a great wine –
how would I know? – but you could taste the soil
crumbling under your tongue. Its musty bucolic core
spoke of antiquity.
                    Only later we learnt
of a loving couple who a few years previously
had fallen head over heels into the well, and drowned.
To this day they had not been recovered; their soft limbs,
entwined in roots perhaps, had thrown
a subtle sediment, making the wine full-bodied.

HI-FI
for Oonagh

Crude as a hippopotamus myself
and for the most part happy in my skin,
how come I live with you, my antibody
and love my antipodes high-wire survival act?
Just let me count the ways.

Your nose, a one-woman bomb-disposal squad,
ransacks the fridge to unearth decaying lettuce,
or disarm fungoid cream cheese. Your ears cringe not only at
the crackle of newspapers but prick up at the slightest
insect scratching at the window pane.
Your radar eyes zero in on the kitchen floor's
grease marks at twenty paces. Your hi-fi taste buds
lay trip wires for blueberries, one-day-old fish.
Your whole body like a barometer responds
to dips and rises in the Humidex,
waxes and wanes with the moon. Like litmus paper,
when air-conditioned you change colour and bask
in cat-like felicity. If only
five senses were enough. But no,
when your psyche's in overdrive
nothing escapes your sixth and seventh senses.
You are like an introverted porcupine.

What a pity the mines are all closing:
You'd have made a first-rate canary.

COUNTRY AND WESTERN

The windshield wipers like a metronome
remind me I'm a thousand miles from home.

With my eighteen-wheeler surging through the night
I've only got my safety belt to hold me tight.

Though the tires keep humming that same old bluegrass tune
I know I'm headed for a blow-out some day soon.

In the crowded diner I listen to the jukebox play
but my mind's freewheeling since you went away.

Flyovers, truck stops, turnpikes all night long,
but my wheels won't take me where my heart belongs.

There's a snowstorm coming, the light on the dash is blue.
All roads are empty till I get back to you.

A MAN OF MANY PARTS

for Antony

Though my dentist tells me my bite is worse than my bark,
my dermatologist insists
my bark needs regular scrubbing.
My chiropractor finds me stiff-necked
yet my cardiologist assures me my heart
is still in the right place.
My optometrist's content with my 20/20 hindsight but claims
that my vision for the future's unsure,
while as for my personal trainer, she says I can stay the course
if it's only one course, of a leaner, meaner cuisine.

As I watch these specialists wheeling
like vultures over me, looking for juicy bits,
I wonder, can only the undertaker
see me whole as I really am,
as he finishes a made-to-measure box
to replace my birthday suit?

WHAT A BUNCH OF IDIOMS!

It's an ill wind that blows nobody light work.
A good wine cannot change its spots.
Look before you spoil the broth.
Every cloud is coming up roses.

A leopard cannot carry coals to Newcastle.
A friend in need needs no bush.
In for a penny, nothing win.
Every dog has a silver lining.

Too many cooks run deep.
A bird in the hand is better than no bread.
Still waters are soon parted.
One man's meat saves nine.

WAITING FOR MR. GUPTA

Up in the Western Ghats,
awaiting calls on our cellphones
from Canada, Ireland, France,
we become unwilling
eavesdroppers, accomplices
in someone's domestic drama.
A female voice won't be persuaded
that Oonagh is not the woman
who now lives with Mr. Gupta,
once her fiancé.
At all hours of night and day,
rehearsing tearful reunions,
she tries to catch us out.
Everyone's disappointed.

ECOLOGY

Unlike oil, natural gas or the Amazon forest,
love is a renewable resource:
drill deep enough and you'll find it still welling up
from the bed of the ocean or flaring across prairie landscapes,
sweet, light, crude, whatever.

A tattered coat

MEMOIR

Even today it can't all be outsourced.
Memoir remains the go-to place for do-it-yourself-ish
down-to-earth recollections. Be wary of those
who want you to splurge on the packaging,
tart up the story with Madison Avenue
birthday frills and bows, gift-wrap your childhood.
Far better botch the job
with Scotch tape and coloured cellophane, untidy knots
that leave a few strands dangling.
There are always odds and ends
lying around that a scavenger so inclined
could easily weave
into quite a different story.

MASKS

Bikers, leather-clad,
are battened behind dark glass
against road dust.
So too welders protect
their eyes from the blue cone
of oxy-acetylene,
and skiers against the snow,
meticulous surgeons,
sheltered and sheltering,
behind goggles, a mask.
Bandits and burglars too,
all this I understand.

But masks of authority,
expressionless, afraid
of losing face,
demand
a transplant of power,
a whole-face lift.
So riot cops, militias,
immune to scrutiny,
are visored in plexiglass,
mediaeval, opaque
to any argument.

This is no tribal rite:
the state asserts itself
through masks that presuppose
absolute control.
Hangmen and torturers
prefer anonymous
hoods, slits only
where eyes should be.
Menace and secrecy
become their own ends.

Yet to make someone human
we need to speak face to face,
see their prismatic eyes,
concentrate
that blue flame
of love, hatred, anger, joy
and for frankness lay aside
too easily assumed
masks of indifference.

Who does not pride himself
on reading faces,
distinguishing between
the Janus replicas?
Yet few truly decipher
the facsimiles of grief
but take at face value
the smiling bland assurance
of diplomats, barristers
who for their own ends trade
upon our naked trust.

In time all will be known,
but maybe not in our time.
Mere husks of what we were,
eroded from within,
we cherish and sustain
each brittle carapace
as we await the death mask's
ultimate travesty.

STICK INSECT

I have seen them in India
almost invisible
against the surrounding twigs.
Now on doctor's orders
I have become one myself,
tripod, trinity, icon
of benign decrepitude,
awkwardly stickhandling
my way as best I can.
My cane, and this scrawny husk,
even at Halloween
afford me no disguise.

HAIR

A stray hair, garnished with
dust, balled up, stockpiled
alongside nail parings, skin
in unseen congested nooks
of bathrooms, stairwells, closets –
how these unsightly reminders
have whittled, reduced me to
a legacy of dust.

So my unnoticed loss
keeps pace with my decline,
expands as I diminish.
These cast-offs, fodder at most
for DNA forensics,
are more than enough
to justify a charge
of criminal negligence,
for growing old so soon
and so untidily.

FINE LINES

Mirrors do not discriminate,
show only surface, moonscapes.
It takes clearer eyes
to see how the pangs of experience
dredge alluvial skin,
whittle us to inscribe
our own fine lines upon
forehead, cheekbone, neck.

Even archeologists,
whose carbon counters prise
well-preserved jaw-bone fragments
out of the African dust,
resetting the human time scale
half a million years further back,
cannot yet reconstitute
one fugitive glance or smile.
We look in the glass and wonder
where has the taut skin vanished,
what made that vein collapse?

Only Rembrandt or Lucian Freud
could treasure for their own sake
the craters, rift valleys, faults,
that make up our personal landscapes.
Though powder may cover up,
air-brush unwanted tears,
and photographers filter out
relics of guilt and grief,
hearts cannot so easily
be lifted: a fine line runs between
acquiescence and despair.
It takes steadfastness to see
time's crewel handiwork
embroidering brow and chin.

SHUT-IN

Time has tricked you again:
in a diagnostic test
a prized kindergarten skill
eludes you now. How can you tell
time that it is all wrong?
Your hands go to your face,
bewildered by the way
some vicious chemistry
has fused memory's cells,
confines you to the past,
while we who shared that past,
what can we do but watch
as through a two-way mirror?

WRAITH

He sits as massive as the granite heads
on Easter Island, smiling. This gentle dignity
was how we'd always known him. He'd patiently explain
some point in epidemiology or watch
his three granddaughters play, or remember Chile –
to all of us a wise and courteous man.

Even before they moved him to the Lodge
he would gaze all day down the well that was his life
and hear no echo as our words splashed. He has become
a child again, but mummified, too large and cumbersome.
We drift like familiars through his waking dream.

Now he's forgotten how to talk, even in Spanish.
Though occasional sunlight infiltrates the clouds
and he grows briefly lucid, mostly like November leaves
his accomplishments fall away from him, he sleeps.
Already with no time left for the impossible
farewell, there's nothing to be retrieved
as the last red lamp at the end of his train of thought
diminishes round a curve into forested dark.

FERRY TERMINAL

Confronting the ocean
startling arcades of light
from afar almost hover
above the shoreline: we gather,
intent on departure, beset
by gantries, stairways, sheds,
a windsock, hawsers –
marine technology's
immaculate white
arenas of emptiness.

Lounging by our bags,
leaving time for the expected
delays, non-arrivals, the brute
rituals of waiting,
we turn to scrutinize
our fellow passengers
or picture through plate glass
who will be waiting there
at the other end to greet us.

A ship's horn, bells, remind us
that journey is still ahead
where massive solitudes
loom out of the mist, dissolve
through bays, coves, hidden inlets,
unseen peninsulas. We'll gaze as
a drift of islands assimilates
into the sleek horizons
settled now by cloud
and the grey slide of the sea.

We must be open to enter
this kingdom of wind and tide
and the water's uncertainty.
In order to set sail
we must believe that further shores exist,
invisible continents.

REACHING THE BLUE HOUSE

It was a long flight eastwards
into the sun, but now touching down
in the hard air of Switzerland,
it is all settled, I am absolved
of the pain of indecision,
my mind grows bright with relief.

An unlikely place it seems
to end my days, among
warehouses, office blocks,
but the blue house, set apart,
may grant some peace at last.

Family and friends
have made me feel at home:
music, bright furnishings,
strong hands, a steadying arm,
and eyes that will hold back tears
till after that last farewell,

when they that are left,
enfolded in memories,
can gaze into a blue
beyond our earthly orbit,
an ocean that yields no wake,
only a chosen calm.

NOTES ON THE POEMS

Berlin Revisited
Judensterne were the yellow cloth stars that the Nazis forced all Jews to wear.
Karl Liebknecht and Rosa Luxemburg were leading German Socialists and revolutionaries. They were both killed in the suppression of the Spartacist uprising of 1919.

Sans Souci
(the name means literally "without a care") was the palace King Frederick the Great of Prussia built for himself at Potsdam.

Renernig
A hamlet in central Brittany. "My all but forgotten father tongue" refers to the fact that my father was born in France, at age twenty became a naturalized Englishman, and taught French for thirty-three years in London but almost never spoke French with my mother or myself at home.

Counterpoint
My main source for details about Brahms' life was Styra Avins' 1997 volume *Johannes Brahms: Life and Letters,* along with Karl Geiringer's *On Brahms and His Circle*, Florence May's two-volume *The Life of Johannes Brahms*, and Michael Musgrave's *A Brahms Reader.* I also consulted memoirs about, and correspondence with, Brahms by Albert Dietrich, Otto Gottlieb-Billroth, George Henschel, Kurt Hofmann, Heinrich and Elisabeth von Herzogenberg, Walter Hubbe, Gustav Ophüls, Nancy B. Reich, Willi Reich, Willi Schramm, Clara Schumann, Rudolf von der Leyen, and Joseph Viktor Widmann.

ACKNOWLEDGEMENTS

Some of these poems have been published in the following magazines: *Dalhousie Review, Event, Kavya Bharata, Malahat Review, The Antigonish Review, The New Quarterly, The Newsletter of the Farewell Foundation,* and *Vallum.* All the poems in the sequence *Getting To Know You: a Vancouver Suite* first appeared in a limited, fine-art edition of the same name accompanied by etchings by Sigrid Albert and printed by Peter Braune at New Leaf Editions. Three other poems reproduced here, "Shell," "A Dog's Life," and "Ferry Terminal," also first appeared in that same volume.

My thanks to Ken Klonsky and other members of A-Drift Writers Collective in Vancouver for their patient critiques of many of these poems and, as always, to Oonagh, my wife, who listens carefully to my newest work and offers sound advice even before breakfast.

Other Recent Quattro Poetry Books